BEFORE YOU GET A PET:

THE ESSENTIAL QUESTIONS TO ASK

BY

TAMMY HAYES

Before You Get a Pet – The Essential Questions to Ask

Published by
T.L. Hayes Enterprises, LLC
It's DogGone Awesome
ItsDogGoneAwesome.com

SBN: 979-8-9998183-1-7

Other books available:

So You Want a Dog: The Six Keys to a Successful Relationship

Keeping Your Pets: 10 Essential Strategies to Care For Your Pet During Difficult Times   (Includes Emergency Preparation)

Stay Pawsitive: Reasons for Pet Surrender and How to Prevent It

Introduction

Every year, new pets are brought into homes with excitement and high expectations. But due to the new owners not considering the questions listed in this small guide, many of those pets are rehomed, relinquished to shelters or rescues, or are abandoned. With advanced considerations and preparation, the transition from being a non-pet household to a pet-owning household can be much smoother and beneficial to both the owner(s) and the pet(s).

There are six important Keys to consider before obtaining any pet. The following sections will describe each Key and give a brief description for it. The questions that come after each Key will enable potential owners to have a more rewarding experience when they bring home a pet, but only if the person considering the questions is honest with the answers. They require the potential new owner(s) to consider the many factors that help create a solid owner/pet bond. These include:

- ability to make a commitment
- individual temperament and personality
- lifestyle and interests
- future plans
- financial situation
- family members that live with them
- living situation

Review the different Keys and answer the questions honestly. There is no right or wrong answer to any of these questions, as it is an individual evaluation. If you have family members or a roommate, consider discussing these questions with them. These questions will help you be more aware of the various aspects of pet ownership and what should be considered before a pet is brought into the home, resulting in a more positive pet owning experience for you and your family.

FIRST KEY – COMMITMENT

Commitment is the first key, as without a solid commitment, the remaining five keys have little meaning. This commitment to the pet will require that you are responsible for the quality care of the chosen pet for the duration of its lifetime, or that you make arrangements in case something happens to you. Keep in mind that some pets, like gerbils, rats, etc., may not have a long lifespan, but others, such as dogs and cats, can live into their teens, and some pets, especially birds, can outlive their owners. This commitment extends to its care on a daily, monthly, and yearly basis, and there are no time-outs or other options, unless you hire a pet sitter or boarding kennel.

Questions to consider:

- Do you have what it takes to be fully committed to your chosen pet for its lifetime?
- Is "now" an appropriate time to bring home a pet?
- Do you have the time to take care of the pet correctly and on a daily basis?
- Are you willing and able to love and care for this pet for its entire lifetime?
- What are your long and short-term goals? How will this affect your pet?
- Is there the possibility of changing employment and how will that affect your life and pet?
- Are you willing to provide your pet with the proper exercise, environment, training, nutrition, and grooming?
- If you are currently single, will you keep the pet even if a new relationship doesn't approve of or like your pet?

- Are you willing to give up some of your free time activities or spur-of-the-moment vacations?
- What arrangements will you make for your pet if you are no longer able to care for him?
- Are you willing to take the time to train the pet correctly, or seek professional help when needed? Or possibly change employment?
- Are you willing to take the risk of not knowing the background of any pet that you get from an advertisement, shelter or rescue, or grocery store parking lot?
- If the pet develops health or temperament issues, will you seek professional help and make decisions based on patience and intelligent research?

SECOND KEY – YOU AND YOUR FAMILY

The owner and family/roommate unit is the second Key. Your personal interests, habits, hobbies and lifestyle will help you decide what type of pet would best suit you. If you have any family, be it a spouse, children, grandchildren, grandparents, or a roommate, their interests, habits, hobbies and lifestyle may influence your choice of pet too, depending on how interactive they will be with the pet.

Children who are raised with pets are frequently more likely to be empathetic, caring and responsible, especially if they have had the duty of taking care of the pet on a regular basis. They also are less likely to develop allergies. Children can benefit from helping to care for the pet, and if it is the right type of pet, they may be able to join an organization like the 4-H or Future Farmers of America and learn valuable skills as an active, participating member.

Any pet that you bring in should not only fit you and your personality, but you should also fit the pet's personality, quirks and temperament. If the family members or a roommate will be involved in the care of the pet, than their individual temperaments and abilities should also be considered. For the well-being of the pet, as well as for your own mental health, choosing the type of pet that will naturally fit into your life and lifestyle is much more rewarding than going with what is popular at any given moment, but does not suit you.

Questions to consider:
- What type of personality do you have?
- What is your lifestyle?

- Are you married, have a family, or a roommate?
- Will the heads of the household agree on the boundaries that need to be set for the pet, as well as any necessary training?
- Are you taking care of an elderly member of the family or someone with disabilities, divergency, or mental health conditions? How will that affect your choice?
- How is your health? Will you be able to physically and emotionally take care of your chosen pet?
- Are there any known allergies for you or your family? If an allergy occurs, how will you handle it?
- Are you planning on having a baby?
- Do you have children at home? Or frequent visits from either the neighborhood or relatives?
- Will you be getting this pet for a child?
  - How old is the child or children?
  - How responsible is the child or children?
  - What will they be required to do
  - Will they be active in the different sports that are available? Or organizations such as 4-H?
  - If they will be participating in any sports, will you as the parent be there to help guide them and support them?

THIRD KEY – FINANCIAL AND LIVING CIRCUMSTANCES

Your financial situation will dictate what you are able or not able to do as a pet owner. Many people own a pet but do not realistically have the finances to take care of it. If an emergency occurs and requires an extensive veterinary visit, it can be stressful when the funds are not available to cover the possible costs. There are pet insurance options that you could look into to help cover any emergencies that may occur. Your overall living situation will also affect what you can do now and in the future. Your home and financial stability is important so that you know that you can care for your pet consistently over the years.

Consider creating a list of potential costs for the initial purchase of the pet, and also the ongoing costs to help decide if this is something that can be done at this time. This would include any veterinary care, pet health insurance, food, supplies and toys.. An alternative to having health insurance would be to have a separate credit card that was only used for the pet. This card would need to have at least a $2,000 or higher limit, depending on the type of pet you have.

Your living circumstances will also dictate whether or not you can bring a pet home at this time. Consider if the home that you currently live in is able to accommodate the pet that you are considering. When looking at your home, take a few minutes to pretend that you have your particular pet. Think of what a normal day would be like; feeding, walking, exercising, cleaning, or any other activity that you may do with the pet. Ask yourself if it feels doable without too much rearranging or reconstruction.

Take the time to research any zoning laws that may affect your decision. Take these into consideration when you are looking into bringing home a pet. Some Home Owner Associations, cities/town, counties or states may have laws that pertain to your chosen pet. Do your due diligence and spend some time to do research on this, as if you are found to be against the laws, your animal can be taken from you and rehomed in a different facility or be euthanized.

Questions to consider:
- What are your living conditions? Do you own or rent?
- Do you plan on moving during the time you have the pet?
- Will your home reasonably accommodate your chosen pet?
- If it is a pet that requires a special habitat, do you have room for it without it becoming an inconvenience?
- Are there any residential rules, city or state regulations or laws that will either allow, with conditions, or prevent you from owning your chosen pet?
- Are there at least two knowledgeable veterinarians available in your area who can take on new clients?

FOURTH KEY – RESEARCH YOUR CHOSEN PET

One of the top reasons that owners rehome or relinquish their pets is because the pet does not fit their personality or lifestyle and they may feel overwhelmed, uninterested, disappointed or unable to provide it the proper care. To avoid this issue, take the time to thoroughly research your pet before you bring one home. Become familiar with the different personalities, quirks, traits, habits and needs that your potential pet may have. Make sure that not only the pet fits into your lifestyle, but that you fit the normal life of the pet. If possible, visit with owners of your chosen pet or see if you can meet them either in a home environment, or outside of the home, to get a feel for the pet and whether or not you believe that you could be comfortable with them in your home. Many owners are more than willing to give you the positives as well as the negatives of owning that particular pet. If you learn of certain traits or issues consistently during your research, be aware that it is most likely something that is "normal" for that pet to do. Decide now, before you have brought home the pet, if that is something that you are okay with. If you have serious doubts, then it may be best if you consider a different pet.'

Questions to consider:

- Are you willing to thoroughly research your chosen pet(s) to learn if it's inherent traits are something that you can live with and that it will suit your regular lifestyle? And that you will suit his?
- Are there any genetic health issues that you should be aware of that may lead to extra veterinary expenses? Are you willing to research any potential health or care

issues so that you will be aware of them and accept the risks?

- If you are considering getting more than one at the same time, or if you are adding a new pet to a household that already has one or more pets or animals, are you willing to work with and train it or keep them separated if needed?
- Are you interested in showing or competing with your chosen pet?
- If yes to the above question, what requirements are there to compete in your chosen sport?
- Are you considering raising/breeding your chosen pet?
    - Are you willing to accept any problems that may arise?
    - Are you willing to be responsible for the progeny, even years later?
    - Are you willing to help new owners and guide them correctly?

FIFTH KEY – LOCATING RESPONSIBLE SOURCES

For the best companion, it is important to know where your pet comes from. The best resource for purebred and health tested pets are breeders who specialize in one particular species or breed. With those companion animals that are able to be health tested and registered, these breeders will know the history of the lines that they use, any potential health issues and the temperament that the pet will most likely have. Keep in mind that with some of the smaller pets, a breeder may have more than one type of pet, but those numbers should be reasonably small and they should be knowledgeable about the different animals and lines that they are using. These are best for those who want to know that the pet they are bringing into their home will have certain traits that they know they can live with. For those who are not as concerned about the traits, shelters and rescues are also a good potential source. Wherever you obtain your pet from, for a longer, happier relationship, it is best to avoid those places that are questionable and may sell unhealthy or sickly animals because they are in it only for the profit, not the animals themselves.

BREEDERS

Breeders should be custodians of their chosen species or breed and strive to do the best that they can do for those animals, as in quality of the new generation, as well as future generations. They are frequently active in the pet world in regards to their specialty, and are members of their species or breed association or club. If there is a standard for their breed, ethical breeders will breed to the standard to maintain the quality of the animals. Take the time to research and locate responsible breeders of your chosen pet. Those who have dedicated themselves to the health and well-being of their pets and the future of those pets are the best sources of information and quality animals. Look for those who perform regular genetic testing on their pets and breed their pets accordingly and do not use those animals that may carry on the genetics that can be harmful to the pet.

Be aware that there are unscrupulous breeders who may sell you an inferior or sick animal. With the internet, there are some who will steal photographs and other information off of other legitimate websites or Facebook and claim it as their own. Be cautious if you are not able to pick the pet up in person, as there have been issues of people not receiving their pet, or not receiving the pet that was agreed upon. While it isn't common, it has happened, so be cautious when dealing with someone on the internet who is not close enough for you to physically visit. Make sure that the person or entity that you are purchasing your pet from is responsible and respectable. You can frequently get to know them through social media, how they respond to you, and how they engage with others.

.Here are some questions that you should consider when researching breeders:

- Can you visit the facilities or home?
- Is the property well taken care of and living quarters clean?
- If a dog, do they use any of the puppy raising programs? Which one and why?
- How much time do they spend with the pets and with the young?
- Can you view and visit with the parents and other pets that are on the property?

- Do they appear well cared for and of appropriate temperament and physical appearance?
- Are there any reviews of the facilities on the internet or in the website communities where they may be found?
- How active are they in their pet communities?
- How long have they been active in the species or breed?
- If there is a registry, are they a member?
- Do they health test their pets, if tests are available?
- How many times do they breed their females, and do they allow a reasonable rest in between? (For example, do they allow the females to rest through one or two heat cycles before breeding again?)
- How many litters do they have a year?
- How much do they charge per young animal? Do they charge a different price per color?
- Do they raise several breeds or species?
- If you are interested in a working dog breed of any kind, are the breeders active in the field that you are interested in? (i.e. – do they work their herding dogs with stock on a regular basis? Do they hunt with their bird dog? Are their hounds hunted with?)

NOTES ON THE ABOVE LIST

Not being "out there" is not a detriment to acquiring a pet from them, but if they are more visible it will give you a clearer idea of who they are and how well they care for their animals and their pet community, education, and future. This will depend on the type of pet you are considering, your location, and what activities are available in your area. Be aware that some breeders may not allow strangers on their property. This is for biosecurity as well as the safety of their animals and premises. In this case, use your best judgment. Look at the photographs that are on their website or personal page. Look also for videos, as those are more difficult to copy and steal from the internet. Are there photos of the family engaged with the pet, such as hiking, playing in the yard, working livestock, napping on the couch with the kids or attending a dog training class? Do the animals look well cared for and are the facilities or living area clean and maintained? Most of the times this will be a residence. Does it look reasonably clean, without junk and debris laying around? When possible, look for referrals. If you join the pet boards or groups, you can learn who is active in the community and they, in turn, can learn more about you and your intentions. Read through their posts on the board. How often do they interact with the people on the board? Do they seem to be helpful and knowledgeable? If it is a Facebook Board, take a look at their personal page and see if their posts on that page reflect what they are promoting. Does their personal page seem to be legitimate, with conversations focusing on their pets or other relevant posts? Avoid those who appear fake or questionable. If you know someone who has the pet that you are interested in, ask them where they obtained their pet and would they recommend them? If the breeder you like is a distance away, ask if they can recommend someone closer. Many breeders are more than happy to refer you to others whom they know personally or have knowledge of. Veterinarians can also be a potential source of responsible breeders, as they will be treating the animals of those people and be familiar with the quality of care and attention that is provided.

You should also expect the breeder to question you and ask why you are interested in their particular pet, what your experience is with pets and this particular one, and if you are prepared to care for it throughout its lifetime. A breeder who is responsible and cares about their pets will encourage you and be available for any questions or concerns that you may have.

SHELTERS AND RESCUES

There are a several types of shelters and rescues throughout the United States and Canada. While the main goals of protecting animals who have lost their home and rehoming those animals is the same, the actual operating status can be very different.

Differences between "No-Kill" Shelters and "Kill" Shelters – By definition, a "no-kill" shelter is required to place at least 90% of the animals under their care into a home. Unfortunately, there is no governing body or regulations that a shelter reports to, as well as no definite laws or rules that are adhered to, so each shelter will have their own set standards to go by. Most do work hard at avoiding euthanizing those animals that are healthy and adoptable, only euthanizing those animals who are terminally ill, untreatable or are considered dangerous to society. There is also a difference on how they acquire their animals. Some shelters have an "open door" policy, where they will not turn away an animal, no matter the condition that the animal is in. Many of the no-kill shelters will have a "closed door" or "limited access" policy, where they will only take in those animals that they deem more likely to be adopted due to health, breed, or temperament.

A "kill" shelter is one who accepts all animals, no matter what the health or temperament is of the pet. They are not able to turn them away, but will bring them into the system and care for them the best way possible. Due to the fact that they are unable to turn away any animal, they become full quickly and in order to assist other intakes, they frequently have to face the decision of making room by euthanasia.

If considering a rescue, be cautious of animals that are imported, as they can carry diseases that can harm them, other pets or people who come in contact with them. Currently, in 2025, dogs brought in for "resale" are exempt from the regulations required of other dogs, according to the APHIS/USDA website on live animal imports. Temperament, breed and background is also an unknown and may or may not be of concern. This will depend solely on the individual owner and dog.

Differences between Breed Rescues and General Rescues – The main difference that can be found in Rescues are whether or not the Rescue will have more of an open-door policy, or if they only take pets from either a certain pet type or one particular breed. Many of the breed registries, clubs and associations have a rescue group within the club that helps rehome pets of that specific breed, or at times, will accept crosses of the breed also. There are "type" of pet rescues, such as bully breed rescues, livestock guardian dog rescues, hunting dog rescues and herding dog rescues. These will take in or assist those pets that are considered a member of that particular type or group. The general rescues will take in or assist those pets that are of any species or breed. While most of these pets are acquired from relinquishments, they will also work with shelters to pull out those breeds or types that correspond with their particular rescue. Some of these rescues may work more on a foster basis, so will not be able to rescue and assist as many pets as others.

Shelters and rescues obtain their animals mainly from strays or owner relinquishments. Both will frequently transport pets to other shelters to help find homes for the pets. Some may be obtained from hoarding or other situations where they rescue the animals from unhealthy living conditions.. While most shelters and rescues are focused on the well-being of the animals in their care, be aware that some may not be as responsible or honest.

Consider these questions when choosing to purchase a pet from a shelter or rescue:

- Ask them where their animals come from
  - Are they strays?
  - Owner relinquished?
  - Picked up on raids?
  - Acquired from other areas, states, or countries?
  - Transferred from another shelter?
- If you can visit the facilities, are they clean?
- Do the animals appear well cared for and healthy?
- How difficult is it for potential adopters to be selected?
- Do they have very stringent qualifications to meet and difficult requirements?
- Or are they reasonable and willing to work with a potential adopter?

- Do they have an educational program?
  - How robust and active is it?
  - Are they actively engaged with the community?
- Are they diligent in testing and learning about each animal resident as best as reasonably possible?
- Do they have a solid foster care program in place, with knowledgeable "parents?"
- Are these foster parents available to help work through some of the possible issues and give insights as to what that pet is like in a "normal" home environment?
- Are they dedicated to matching the available pet with the right potential adopter?
- How long have they been in operation?
- Can you find reviews online?
- If something prevents you from keeping the pet in the future, are you able to return it?
- Are they willing to help you with any issues and exhaust all possibilities to solve them?

Shelters and rescue organizations can be a good potential source for your new pet. Those specializing in only one particular breed can offer the potential new owner more specific information and can be a good source in the adopting and adapting process that each owner and pet will require. County and city shelters can also offer quality information to help make the adoption and adapting period go smoothly if they have a solid community education program in place.

If you are looking only for a companion, there are many shelter animals who may do very well for you. Be aware though that as these animals usually come from unknown backgrounds, you will have no idea of health or temperament problems that they may have. While the shelter workers do the best that they can, any animal is an unknown as to breed and age. As they can only go by looks, and somewhat on temperament, the breeds listed can be right or wrong. For example, a pet that looks like a certain breed may also have another breed crossed into it, but it inherited the build and coat genes more from the one parent than the other. If the breed is known, the new pet owner will have a better idea of what to expect from that pet in regards to temperament and inherited instincts. Keep in mind that potential health issues can remain hidden, especially in a young animal. Understandably, there is no health testing in shelter animals as there are in responsibly bred pets, so there is a higher risk. This is not to say that the pet will eventually have a health issue, but it is better to be aware of that potential and plan ahead. If you purchase a pet from a shelter or rescue, you can have a DNA test done by those companies that offer these tests. You most likely will receive different answers as to which breed(s) may be in your pet, or what potential health issues may be inherited by your pet, but it will give you a guideline to start with.

PET SHOPS AND PET STORES

Pet shops have become synonymous with puppy mills and very poorly bred and sickly animals, as well as questionable care of the animals in their facilities. While it is not right to judge all pet shops and pet stores under the same bad label, care must be taken when considering acquiring a pet from a pet shop. There are no federal laws or regulations that regulate pet stores, and under the USDA Animal Welfare Act, most retail stores are exempt. Each individual state may have animal welfare or Pet Animal Care laws on the books that the pet shops must adhere to. The USDA does have requirements for pet breeders to be licensed, and their facilities inspected, but that does not guarantee that the animals are well cared for and the facilities are suitable for the pets. Most pet stores acquire their pets, of all kinds, from these types of facilities, where there is little oversight on the quality of the living conditions, feed, or care. Health and breeding for quality temperament is frequently not addressed in these mills. Also, genetics and the health of the pets is not a matter of importance. A large percentage of the mills are strictly there for the profit they can gain from breeding and selling the progeny, with substandard care being the norm. Also, the pets frequently live in substandard living conditions, and are not allowed to have quality of life and do not interact with the owner. There is a very small percentage that are actually interested in the welfare of the pets they obtain. These breeders are very dedicated to providing healthy pets and also educating the public about the pets they provide.

Proceed with caution when obtaining a pet from a pet store. Look for clean and appropriate cages and enclosures. Keep in mind though, that you are not able to see the back rooms, and while the store floor may be clean and neat, there is no guarantee that the back is also. Talk with the employees and store owner if possible and inquire where they obtained their animals. Ask them questions about the health of their pets, about veterinarian care and visits, health guarantees and educational information. If you can find out the name of the veterinarian, you could consider contacting them and verifying that they visit the store regularly for pet care. Do the employees seem to be knowledgeable and helpful, without avoiding questions or eye contact? Do they seem honest and sincere? Do they ask you what you know about your particular choice of species or breeds and offer good, solid information and recommendations? Do the pets seem confidant and comfortable or are they shy, skittish, and nervous around people? Do they seem to want to provide healthy, well taken care of pets who are suitable as a pet for the average owner? Do they have community classes to help beginner pet owners learn more about their particular pet and how to best care for it?

Frequently, the young animals may not have their age appropriate shots and are sick when the unsuspecting new owner takes one home. Learn which shots are required for your pet, and at what age. Ask for a record of all shots given to the pet and inquire as to which veterinarian they use. You may consider finding a different veterinarian to have the young animal thoroughly checked for any potential issues to avoid any prejudice.

Many states have created laws to prohibit pets from being sold at pet stores. These stores have begun to bring in pets from local rescues and shelters for adoption. If the pet store you are visiting offers this, verify what rescue or shelter they are working with and that the pets are legitimately rescues.

OTHER SOURCES

One can easily acquire a pet from numerous other sources, mainly Craig's List, Facebook Marketplace, internet pet boards, local newspapers or want ads, or the neighborhood grocery store parking lot. With any of these sources, use caution. While most of these pets are legitimately owned and offered for sale, or free, by the person who has them, there have been cases of pet theft and fraud. Ask the same questions as with the breeders, and if possible, see the facilities and parents. Paperwork may or may not be available, and veterinary care may or may not have been done. Ask for any paperwork for shot records and who the veterinarian was, Make sure to contact them to verify the information. If it is an animal that can have health tests of the parents, ask if that has been done and any paperwork available as proof. Use caution and discretion with any of these sources, and if you have any doubts, do not take the pet home.

TIPS ON HOW TO ACQUIRE THE PET

- Do your research. Do not take the short cut.
- Join groups on Facebook and other social media where people discuss the species or breed you are researching and share valuable information and experiences.
- If possible, meet several of your chosen pet or breed in their home environment or at shows and have an honest talk with the owners
- Look for associations, clubs or registries and join them, and if possible, participate in their activities
- Once you have decided on what species or breed you want, locate a reliable source:
    - Members of the clubs, associations, or registries (some have a Code of Ethics that breeders are required to sign)
    - Look for quality, reliable shelters or rescues
    - Talk with others who have the breed you are interested in and ask where they acquired theirs and what their experiences were
    - When possible, check if there are any reviews available of the person or place that you are considering
- When actually picking out the pet, make sure that it is alert, active, well-socialized, has bright eyes, that it is clean, appears to be well fed and taken care of and the environment appears to be maintained, as well as the parents if you are able to see them
- Make sure that the temperament and characteristics of the pet appears to be what one would expect from that particular type of pet

- Make sure to obtain any health certificates and registration papers if applicable

SIXTH KEY – LIVING WITH A PET

Living with a pet will bring on new challenges, which will change to other challenges as the pet goes through adolescence, maturity, and then senior ages. Most of these can be less of a challenge if proper exercise, training, shelter, nutrition, and grooming are included in the day-to-day life of the owner and pet. This is because the owner and pet will grow together and accept the changes and acknowledge them as they come. When you are more hands-on with raising and living with the pet, you will come to understand the pet and expect certain behaviors, which will allow you to create a closer bond.

EXERCISE

Proper exercise is very important, both physically and mentally. Even your smaller pets can benefit from some type of exercise that is designed specifically for them. Mental challenges can tire them out in a different way than physical activity. Both are important to keep your pet content and well adjusted. Many pets can be trained a variety of different tricks, which helps them develop more self-control and confidence. If you have a food or toy motivated pet, training will be much easier. Pets who are not food or toy-motivated will require more ingenuity from you to find ways to encourage them to listen to you and learn. Pets who have a more dominant temperament may need to be shown why these exercises are necessary or they will be reluctant to participate. Remember to always keep it fun, upbeat, and positive. The length of the training sessions and activity level should correspond with the individual pet in regards to age and mental maturity.

ENVIRONMENT

A clean, sheltered environment will help keep your pet feeling safe and content. It is preferable for the pet to be in the house with you unless you are considering a livestock guardian dog or other working animal. If the pet is to be outside for any time, make sure that they always have access to clean, potable water as well as a shelter that will provide relief from the sun, wind, rain, snow, heat, and cold. While many of the animals that were bred to be outside may not use it, instead preferring to sleep out in all sorts of weather, they should have that option. Depending on where you live, you may be restricted as to how much time your pet is allowed to live outside and what provisions are provided for him. Check with your local laws to see what may be required in your area. While there is no Federal Law for how you house your pet, there may be laws in place in each state, county or city. Take the time to investigate any laws that may pertain to you and your pet before you acquire it.

Provide your pet with an area where he can retreat if the activity level is too high for him, and make sure that all of those in the household respect the pet's desire to be left alone. Decide before you bring your pet home whether or not they will be allowed on the furniture or on your bed. Chances are good that you will change your mind if at first you think "no pets on the furniture," but establish that rule early, so that it is you making the decision. Consider also the adult size of the pet and if your current living conditions will accommodate it adequately and allow the pet room to move freely without being cramped in too tight of a space. Make sure that the environment is safe, with no small places that small pets could squeeze into and become stuck, or dangerous items that could fall on them or lacerate them. Be aware of any plants, either inside or outside, that could be potentially lethal if the pet chews on it. To avoid damaged electric cords, move them out of the way or if necessary, run them through a tube so that the pet cannot easily access them and chew on them. If someone in the household uses an inhaler, keep it in a place where the pet has no access to it, as the smell can attract the pet, but the product inside can kill it. Consider any other item that you may have in your household and research anything that you feel may be a threat to your pet. As the pantry area can provide many things for a pet to get into, make sure that it cannot access the food storage area. This is especially true if there is the potential for any foods that may contain xylitol or any of the artificial sweeteners that are similar to it. Xylitol is deadly to pets and if ingested, can quickly lead to an unpleasant death. (Xylitol and other artificial sweeteners can be found in a wide variety of foods like peanut butter, or even non-food items such as toothpaste. Be aware of the potential harm that it can cause, read your labels carefully and keep any xylitol or artificial sweeteners locked up and inaccessible.)

NUTRITION

Proper nutrition is very important. Providing clean water and appropriate nutritious food will help your pet thrive and live a longer life. You may want to research and learn more about what types of food are best for your pet and where you can purchase it. Consider consulting with your veterinarian concerning proper nutrition, although some are not open to options other than commercial pet food. Proper and nutritious food will help prevent the pet from becoming sick, which helps you save on veterinary costs. Learn to read and understand the nutrition labels on the pet food. Ingredients are listed according to weight, with the heavier items listed first, then the lesser weights listed in the appropriate order. It would be advisable to discuss this with a holistic veterinarian or your own veterinarian if he supports homemade or raw feeding for pets, if you are interested in providing a holistic diet. Understanding what is in your pet's food can help you maintain his overall health. Be aware of the nutrition and ingredient label of the treats that you purchase for him also. Many treats contain ingredients such as propylene glycol, BHA, high fructose corn syrup, artificial coloring, ethoxyquin, meat meal, meat by-products and flavor enhancers, none of which are healthy for the pet. One thing to keep in mind is if you can't pronounce it nor know what it is, then it is a good possibility that it is not a healthy ingredient for your pet. Remember that most pets are fed basically the same foods day in and day out, so any of these ingredients that may be harmful to the pet will build up in their system and can cause serious health issues as the pet ages.

GROOMING

All pets will require some grooming. While the requirements will vary depending on the type of pet, all will need some attention to grooming. Before acquiring your specific pet, take the time to research what type of grooming the pet will require and decide if you are comfortable with its requirements. Grooming can include brushing, bathing, nail and beak trimming. Some pets can be relatively easy to keep well-maintained, while others will require more attention, time, and potentially financial resources. Some dog breeds will require regular visits to a professional groomer, so it is important to locate a quality groomer who you can feel comfortable leaving your pet with regularly.. Pet's nails need to be trimmed on a regular basis to help maintain the integrity of their feet. Learn how to trim your pet's nails, and beak if you have a bird, by asking your veterinarian to show you how, asking the breeder or shelter/rescue staff, or professional videos on YouTube.

TRAINING

All pets should have at least some basic training. All pets can be trained something, even if it is something small. Working with your pet to teach it commands, such as obedience work, or tricks, can be very rewarding and is worth your time. This adds to your quality time with your pet and can help create a strong bond between you and the pet. Any time spent in training will help you better understand your pet, as you learn more about how he thinks, how he reacts, and what to expect from him as you build your relationship with him. He in turn will learn more about you and be able to interact with you in a better way, and understand what you ask or need. All training should be positive, with you as the owner learning how to give and take and have patience with the pet. It should also be consistent, using the same word and cue each time. Some will be very eager to work with you and look forward to each session. Other pets will require more patience and creative thinking and present more of a challenge. Make sure that your expectations do not overwhelm the pet, and that they are in line with the personality and temperament of the pet.

Keep in mind that many pets will go through their adolescent stage. This time period will depend on the individual pet, but can frequently be equated to the "teenage" years of humans. This is when the pet is becoming sexually mature and growing into adulthood. During this time period, the pet may be more difficult to handle and not react as he had previously to your commands or training. It is important for you as the owner to recognize that this is just a phase and not an indication of what he will be as an adult. At this time, his brain development is going through a stage where the pet may take more risks, but can be more reactive or emotional. Continue to work with him, change up your training methods if needed, and talk with an experienced pet trainer if you feel that your methods are not working. This is the age where many pets are relinquished, abandoned, or become strays as they present more of a challenge then many people know how to deal with. With awareness of this time period, and plans of how to work around it and adjust your expectations, you and your pet can get passed this stage in his life. With patience, this stage of life will pass and you will develop a strong relationship with your pet for the duration of its life.

CONCLUSION

If you honestly work through this booklet, take the time to consider each question, envision what your life will be like with the possible pet, then you will be richly rewarded for the life of that pet.

The time that you spend now on considering these questions, will help you to avoid any problems and issues in the future. As you read through and answer them, you will start to see a pattern develop of what type of pet will fit best in your life. You will be better prepared to provide a home for the right kind of pet, that will suit not only you, but that you will also suit the pet. This will result in a rewarding experience, one that you can share with your family and friends, and may well impact your life for the good.

Following are blank pages for each of the Six Keys which will allow you to write thoughts and notes while reading through the different questions. Make use of this as the thoughts and ideas are fresh in mind and refer to it often as you begin your search for the perfect pet that will be joining you soon.

NOTES FOR FIRST KEY – COMMITMENT

NOTES FOR SECOND KEY – YOU AND YOUR FAMILY

NOTES FOR THIRD KEY – FINANCIAL AND LIVING CIRCUMSTANCES

NOTES FOR FOURTH KEY – RESEARCH YOUR CHOSEN PET

NOTES FOR FIFTH KEY – LOCATING RESPONSIBLE SOURCES

NOTES FOR SIXTH KEY – LIVING WITH A PET

ABOUT THE AUTHOR
AND IT'S DOGGONE AWESOME

Ms. Hayes's love and fascination with dogs started early in her life. She distinctly remembers memorizing the AKC breed standards from a set of encyclopedias when she was only 7 or 8 years old. She also wrote down all the dog breeds she wanted from a large dog breed book that covered approximately 300-400 breeds, which she found in the reference section of the school library in 4th grade.

Her first dog was a mutt that she rescued from the shelter with her graduation money. But as her true love was, and still is, Australian Shepherds, in the mid-80s, she was able to acquire her first purebred Aussie. He was her constant companion, as she tried out conformation, obedience, agility, therapy work, and herding.

She spent time volunteering at the Salt Lake County shelter in Utah, and was a member of the Humane Education Awareness Advisory Board. She also pet-sat, worked at a stable on weekends, bought and trained her first horse, volunteered with an equine therapy program as a side walker, had a small ranch with cattle, equines, chickens, dogs, and cats, and also worked for a publisher who published non-fiction dog and horse books.

While volunteering as a rescue representative for the Australian Shepherd, as a member of the Australian Shepherd Club of America, she was saddened by the number of people who wanted to rehome their dogs and the reasons for it. She also observed that many times people brought the wrong type of dog home, mostly out of ignorance, and were unable to handle the dog.

Out of this has grown It's DogGone Awesome. The goal of It's DogGone Awesome is to have all shelters across the country be at a very low 20% of capacity by 2035. To obtain this goal, she will be providing books, educational material, games for people, and interactive games for the various pets.

After observing that there are no books that honestly help people make the right choices, she wrote down the main aspects that people should seriously consider before bringing home any type of pet. *So You Want a Dog – The Six Keys to a Successful Relationship* is the first book to come out of this, with the main goal of helping people learn what they should consider before bringing home any pet. She hopes that after reading this book and the following books that she is writing, people will begin to make the right choices, and fewer pets will be in shelters, be abandoned, or languish in the wrong home with unhappy owners who do not understand them.

A website has been set up that will offer information and links to help people interact more effectively with their pets, as well as offering links to social assistance, such as pet food banks, assistance for medical care and housing, domestic abuse assistance, training links, advice on how to locate professional trainers and behaviorists, pet sitters, and boarding kennels.

www.ingramcontent.com/pod-product-compliance
Lightning Source LLC
Chambersburg PA
CBHW061756040426
42447CB00011B/2323